Birthdays Are a Blessing

Written by Tiffany Magierowski

Illustrated by Alena Karabach

For Casey, who will be forever 28

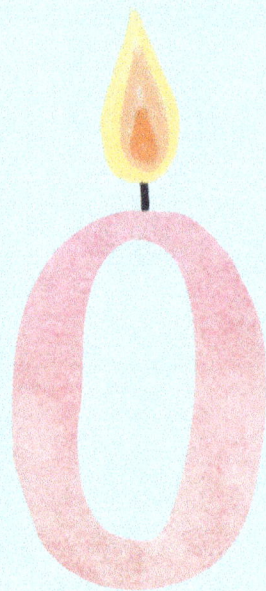

Hello! Welcome to the world!

Pink or Blue?

Either way,

it's nice to meet you!

Enjoy the sweet snuggles in

mom and dad's arms

as they tell you stories about

holidays, trucks, and farms.

The time has passed quickly,

you grew and grew and grew.

Oh, my stars!

Now you are two!

Enjoy the sweet snuggles in

mom and dad's arms

as they tell you stories about

holidays, trucks, and farms.

The time has passed quickly,

you grew and grew and grew.

Oh, my stars!

Now you are two!

Birthdays are a blessing

Birthdays are divine

There's so much to do

And so little time

Oh, wow!

The toddler years

have gone by so fast.

Two, three, four.

Soak it all in,

it won't last.

Your next birthday

is about to arrive.

Oh, goodness!

Now you are five!

Birthdays are a blessing

Birthdays are divine

There's so much to do

And so little time

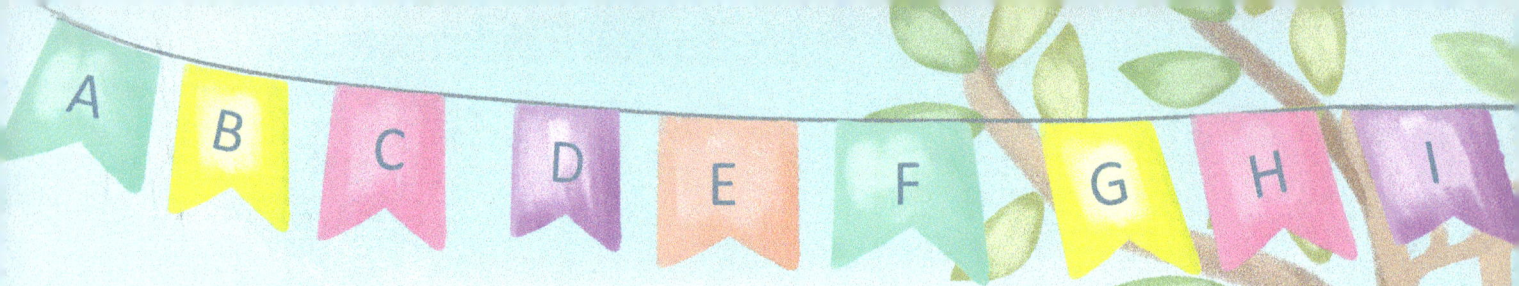

No way!

Off to kindergarten

you must go.

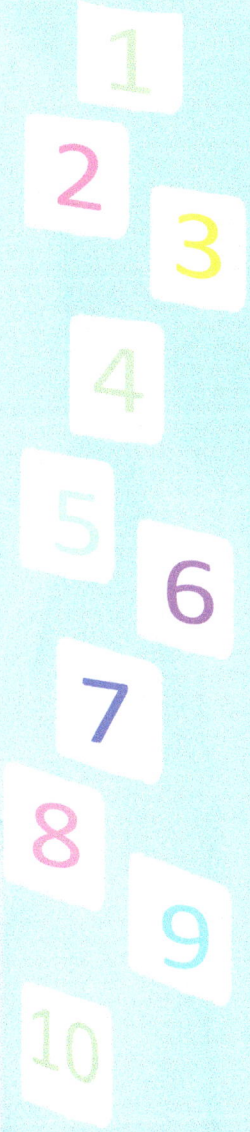

They will attempt to keep

a big smile on their faces and

not let their

true feelings show.

Oh, my heavens!

Now you are seven!

Get ready for friends,

cake, balloons,

and fun.

Congratulations!

You just made another

trip around the sun.

HAPPY BIRTHDAY!

My, oh my!

Now you are nine!

You precious,

precious child,

it's your time

to shine.

In nine more years,

you will be living apart.

sigh
be still my heart

Birthdays are a blessing

Birthdays are divine

There's so much to do

And so little time

Wow!

Eighteen?

Wait.

How did this happen?

It feels like just yesterday,

you were sitting on their laps

smiling and clapping.

Oh, dear.

Your twenties are here.

A time to discover who you are.

Don't worry,

they will always be near.

Never too far.

Heads up!

It's a big world out there.

Be kind, true to yourself,

and strive to be fair.

Birthdays are a blessing

Birthdays are divine

There's so much to do

And so little time

Whew!

Thirty, Forty, Fifty, Sixty.

These years have certainly

gone by quickly.

Remember to look

to the years ahead

with anticipation,

never dread.

HOPE

SMILE

LOVE

Seventy, Eighty, Ninety,

One-Hundred!

Truly, what a gift.

LIVE

FORGIVE

LAUGH

CHERISH

DREAM

Be grateful for all things

big and small

you have been fortunate

to not have missed.

Oh, good grief.

Time is a thief.

There's so much to do . . . . . .

And so little time . . . .

www.ingramcontent.com/pod-product-compliance
Lightning Source LLC
Chambersburg PA
CBHW041601260326
41914CB00011B/1339